JACK

Draw. ~~~~~ ~~ng

50p

Jack
Henderson

HODDER

hodderchildrens.co.uk
jackdrawsanything.com

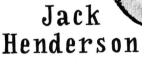

*The Sick Kids Friends Foundation, charity number SC020862, will receive a share of profits from this book, with a minimum donation of £4000.

Idea, design, colours, words, drawings and hard work by me, JACK HENDERSON.

I got lots of help from my mummy, little brother Toby, wee brother Noah & grumpy daddy.

Don't steal my pictures or else I'll become a lawyer when I grow up.

First published in Great Britain in 2011 by Hodder Children's Books

1

A Catalogue record for this book is available from the British Library

ISBN: 978 1 444 90747 6

Creative design and illustration: Paul Cherrill for Basement68

Editorial direction: Sara O'Connor

Printed in Italy

The paper and board used in this paperback by Hodder Children's Books are natural recyclable products made from wood grown in sustainable forests. The manufacturing processes conform to the environmental regulations of the country of origin.

Hodder Children's Books
a division of Hachette Children's Books
338 Euston Road, London NW1 3BH
An Hachette UK company
www.hachette.co.uk

To Toby & Noah

You were too little to really get involved but we were glad you were along for the ride. Love Jack, Mum and Dad

#109: Toby & Noah riding Lots-O'-Huggin' Bear (Lotso) & Rhino for Toby (Jack's little brother)

In Jack's Words

I had been a little bit naughty. I was mean to my brothers Toby and Noah, and Daddy had had enough. "You are NOT going to Grandma and Grandad's house for the afternoon," Daddy said, which made me sad.

Off I went to the craft fair in Haddington. Daddy was at the jumble stall and Mummy was selling her red & rosy crafts. She had let me take my pens and notepad so I was not too bored. I saw Daddy selling old toys so I decided to sell one of my pictures to Anne, Mummy's friend. Anne gave me 20p. I remembered that Daddy was always doing silly things to raise money for charity. He ran a marathon with Uncle Chris, did an obstacle course and jumped off a lighthouse. So I had an idea.

Noah, Jack and Toby

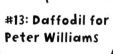

#13: Daffodil for Peter Williams

4

#133: Happy goat for Thomas Jennings

I could draw more pictures in exchange for donations to the Sick Kids Hospital. They are always looking for new toys and machines to help the sick babies. I have been there because I broke my thumb. My brother Toby cut his head at Easter and got an Easter egg. And my little brother Noah has been there lots.

Noah got very sick when he was little and now a cold or cough makes it very hard for him to breathe and he needs to go to hospital right away. He gets oxygen and lots of other different medicines. Daddy says Noah has been admitted eleven times, even though he is only two years old. Every time he goes in I think he is going to die.

If you are reading my book, thank you! You have already helped the Sick Kids a little. But if you want to help out more, visit my website jackdrawsanything.com where you can donate.

Jack Henderson

Noah Henderson is one of 100,000 children from all over the east of Scotland cared for every year at the Royal Hospital for Sick Children in Edinburgh. The Sick Kids Foundation is dedicated to raising funds for the hospital.

As well as providing the very best in medical equipment and facilities, the Sick Kids Friends Foundation aims to give small extra comforts and moments of entertainment for the children that come to stay here. Children don't realise that every hour of painting, drawing or playing with dough contributes significantly to their recovery. Things like welcome presents, special relaxing lights and sounds, and Clowndoctor visits all create an atmosphere where they can relax and enjoy some normal playtime away from the sometimes gruelling medical routine.

Jack #123

#123: Happy girl with a super leg for Ruby

6

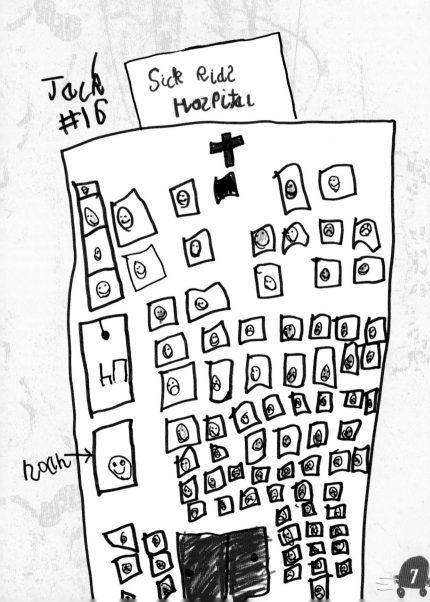

7

The Jack Draws Anything project is a perfect example of how creativity and art can help people heal, and bring people together to support each other in difficult times. As I write this, large display cases are being installed in each of the playrooms and on the main hospital staircase to showcase artworks created by the children. It will be known as Jack's Gallery. Funds raised from this book will enrich our established artistic environment by funding future creative activities throughout the wards.

Jack wanted to say thank you for the care his brothers received, but we cannot thank him and his family enough for the time and talent he has given to raise well over £20,000. From all of us at the Sick Kids Friends Foundation, a huge thank you to Jack and his family, whose inspirational fundraising idea has proven priceless.

Maureen Harrison, Chief Executive
The Sick Kids Friends Foundation

#20: Owl, bike
and pink wellies
for BBC Scotland

8

#176: Clowndoctor for Fiona Carr (Hearts and Minds)

Jack #176

The Clowndoctors visit Sick Kids Hospital every week and receive funding from the Sick Kids Friends Foundation. We wanted to support a wee boy who was doing an amazing job for an amazing charity. - Fiona

#149: Hamburger Man and Hotdog Lady on a date for Scot Carlson

Jack #1

I saw the link in Jack's dad's Twitter feed. Being particularly fond of great ideas, I thought Jack's was a corker and felt compelled to get involved. The picture was for my friend Jenner, whose childhood dream was to swim in a pool of jelly. And the dinosaur? Everyone likes dinosaurs. - Lauren

The Idea

Jack had been fighting with his brothers, Toby and Noah, all morning, and no amount of his mum and dad asking him to stop would make him understand that he was really annoying them. Jack knew that Mum had to go to work at the craft fair, that Dad was going along too, and, as far as he knew, he was going to and spend the afternoon with his grandparents. But because he was being so naughty, his punishment was that he had to go with Mum and Dad to work. But the punishment wasn't going according to plan.

#6: Upchuck for Euan Selkirk

Jack #6

#7: A blue car for Hannah Baker

Jack #7

Once the car was all packed full of pre-loved toys and clothes and Mum's handmade gifts, there was an excited little face peeking out from the back. Jack knew that some of Mum and Dad's friends were going to be there. There would be lots of people to talk to, lots of goodies to buy and, most importantly, since Mum's friends were running the café part, cake!

Inside the old building of the Haddington Corn Exchange, Jack stood at his mum's stall with his drawing pad and pens. He wanted to draw a picture of what he thought the stall should look like. Then he wanted to place the picture on the stall. Mum asked him not to, but he started to move her felt box frames onto the floor to make a space. His mum asked him not to again, but Jack was a very determined little boy. Finally, his mum decided to send him over to the stall his dad was running, selling pre-loved baby items, and give her some peace.

JACR
#2

"What a hero! Noah is lucky to have a big brother like you looking out for him and your mum and dad must be so proud."

Donation by Kevin Thomson

Jack #11

"Thank you to Jack. You are an inspiration to young and old."

Donation by Susanne Jones

Off he plodded, pencil case in hand, head down, mumbling about how mean his mum was. He decided he was going to sell his picture, as it was so great. Five minutes later he ran back over to his mum with a huge smile on his face. His mum's friend Anne Thomson had just paid him 20p for his picture!

Jack used the money to get himself a nice bun from the café and no one thought any more of it until later that day. Jack's dad is a website builder and often helped with his mum's gifts website. They were discussing some new things to add to the red & rosy site, when Jack proclaimed, "I need a website!" Dad was always keen for new projects so decided to humour Jack and sat him down at the little table, got his notepad, cup of coffee, juice for Jack and had a little meeting with him.

Actual meeting notes

#63: Flowers for David's Granma's 90th birthday

At first Mum was a little mad as Dad was not talking about her website any more, but over the course of the next half an hour, her mood soon changed.

Jack wanted a website that he could put his pictures onto and sell. Dad wrote it all down and asked him many questions. He explained what a logo was, how websites work and how people could pay the money. Jack even worked out all the information he would need from someone to draw their picture.

#55: Starfish family on the beach for Katherine Gray

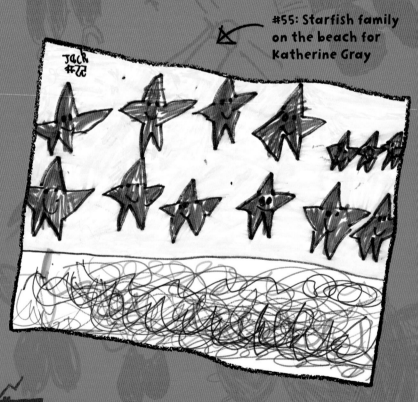

Jack
2E

Lucas wanted a picture of the Gruffalo
drawn for his room. His parents attempted
this - badly - so were delighted to discover,
when Toby and Noah were over playing,
that their big brother draws anything.

Jack
#27

Charlie's brother Rory has the same condition as Noah and has had about eleven stays at the Sick Kids. Rory loves dinosaurs like Toby.

- Gail Prentice, Charlie & Rory's Mum

Then, Jack had an even better idea. He looked at Dad and said, "Could we send the money to charity rather than me keep it?" Mum looked at Dad with a nice smile on her face. Dad smiled back. "Of course you can," they said. Dad asked Jack what charity he would like and they talked about all the things that were special to him. There was, of course, Tiggywinkles (the Hedgehog charity) and the SSPCA (to help animals) but Jack was adamant that he wanted to raise money for the Sick Kids, which is the hospital where he and his brothers, especially Noah, go. Noah has a condition called bronchiolitis that can make breathing difficult sometimes.

So there it was. Jack wanted to draw pictures in exchange for donations to the Sick Kids Friends Foundation. What a lovely simple idea. Dad and Mum were very proud of this idea. They thought they could send it round to family and friends, and maybe raise £100 or so.

#96: Teddy for Evie

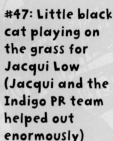

#47: Little black cat playing on the grass for Jacqui Low (Jacqui and the Indigo PR team helped out enormously)

Over the course of the next couple of hours, Mum looked after Noah and Toby while Dad and Jack got to work. They got out their big pens and notepads and proceeded to come up with a name – "Jack Draws Anything". (The first attempt was Jack's Pictures of Anything.) Jack designed a logo – a hedgehog, his favourite animal, with six pens for prickles (Jack was six years old) and they wrote some words for the website. Jack also picked the colours, fonts and decided the best place to put everything.

Jack was very excited and off he went to bed full of ideas. Later that night, Dad built Jack's website as he had requested and put it onto the Internet. This was 21 March 2011 at 10am. The next morning, when Jack saw it, he was super excited. Jack wanted everyone in the world to see his page and how right he was. Life was about to change … for ever.

My name is Georgia and I'm in Jack's class. Jack is my friend and I wanted him to draw a picture of us. The Edinburgh Sick Kids fixed my leg and I just wanted to say a huge thanks to everyone who helped me get better.

#29: JustGiving logo, drawn in and around for Jack Sheldon (JustGiving)

Jack
#2P

Noah

Toby

Jack decided to share this one with his little brothers, **Toby** (3) and **Noah** (1) so they **ALL** had a shot at colouring in. They loved joining in and copying their big brother. JustGiving are the fantastic team that collected our donations online and passed them to the Sick Kids.

Jack #33

"My little boy, also named Jack, was in a Special Baby Unit for a week after he was born with a serious illness, so I like what you're doing. Well done!"

Donation by Dave & Katie Morris

Jack Goes Viral

That morning Jack set the target at £100, which his mum and dad thought was a realistic amount for a six-year-old to raise. Mum and Dad put a link to the new website onto their Facebook, Twitter and LinkedIn pages and off they went to work, school and all the normal things.

Almost instantly, things started to happen. News of Jack's story and generosity was being shared from family to family and person to person. Picture requests and money started to come in, and within four hours Jack had raised his target of £100 and had not even done a single drawing. He was still at school! When he got home that afternoon, he got to work drawing and word continued to spread. Within a day, Jack had reached his new target of £500 and within 2 days he had reached £1,000.

#102: Me playing bass for my new CD cover for Tom Bowers

Jack #102

JaCk
#118

#113: Mr Bump
(from the Mr Men)
for Charlotte Easen

Four days after the website went up, Jack's mum
and dad couldn't believe it when they got a call from STV
(Scottish ITV); a news channel wanted to do a piece on
Jack and his drawing. He already had more than a hundred
picture requests. The next day Liz Monaghan and her
cameraman, Steve Kydd, came to the house before school and
spent some time with Jack, Toby and Noah. This was the first
time Jack introduced himself in his own unique way. He was s
excited that people from the TV were coming to his house tha
he opened the door and said, "Hello, I'm Jack from Jack Draw
Anything!" Then Jack did some drawing and made a lovely pic
for the STV news.

Among all the excitement, Noah was starting to get ill.
As the morning went on, he needed his blue inhaler, was
very sleepy and didn't want to join in at his Jo Jingles
music and dancing class, which was most unlike him.

Jack #36

Jack's vibrant pictures leapt from the page
and made me smile. I thought it was such
a brilliant idea. It was even more lovely as
it was solely Jack's idea as a way of saying
thank you to the hospital that helped
his brothers. - Nicola

#37: Uncle Johnny up the ladders on his fire engine fighting a fire breathing dragon for Aunt Kirstie, Uncle Johnny, Sam and Libby

"You are less than half my age, yet I want to be just like you when I grow up. You are a great inspiration. Keep up the amazing work :)"

Donation by H

30

Where Jack lives, schools finish at twelve noon on a Friday, so Mum picked up Jack and came back home for a quiet afternoon after the madness of the morning. But a BBC reporter, Gavin Walker, and a cameraman were waiting at the house, asking if they could come and film a little segment. At first, Mum wanted to tell them no, but Jack was keen and they said it would be ten minutes.

An hour later, they left. The kids were shattered, Mum was shattered and she wondered if she had done the right thing in letting them do another news report. Little did Mum realise that the piece that Gavin put together was so fantastic that it would lead to bigger and better things. His piece was aired on BBC News 24, CBBC, and BBC Breakfast. In what was an amazing day, Jack's story appeared on both the evening news on STV and BBC Scotland. He made the front page of the *Edinburgh Evening News* and had articles in the *Scottish Sun* and the *Daily Record*.

Jack#128

#125: Owl with giant head and tiny body for Elisa Begg

It all led to the most amazing social networking Internet response that Jack's dad had ever seen. The speed at which Jack's website was shared on Facebook, LinkedIn and especially Twitter was nothing short of incredible. In fact, Jack's mum and dad had spent the majority of their time over that week answering emails, dealing with the press and, most importantly, ensuring Jack wasn't over-worked or made to do something he didn't want to. They would not be responsible for killing his love of drawing. Also, Mum and Dad wanted to make sure that all of their boys were part of this experience, including Toby, the middle monkey, who was three.

But the hardest part was that Noah had spent the last twenty-four hours on the verge of being admitted to the Sick Kids hospital. He was struggling to breathe, his temperature was high and he wasn't able to sleep. Jack's mum and dad were also having a sleepless night.

#122: (Flying) pig for Krista MacKellaig

Jack #122

Jack #48

"Your personality shines through in your artwork - bright, happy and just lovely!! xx"

Donation by Kirsty Lauder

JACK'S FAVOURITE

JaCK#21

We asked for a bumblebee because one of Ethan's very first words was 'buzz'. - Ethan, Suzanne (Auntie Suz!) and Chris Green (Uncle Chris!)

Five days in, Jack's dad sent out a message to all the new fans of Jack and his website:

So, given all of this, and us being a normal family (Dad working, Mum raising the kids and running her own wee business), trying to raise 3 young children while working and sheer overwhelming response and requests, please bear with us. We will reply to every email and every text/tweet as soon as we can. If we miss one out, don't be mad, just let us know. Our initial estimate of 3 days to get a picture onto the website is no longer anywhere near valid and we are looking at ways to keep everyone happy and the fun continuing.

Jack's Dad (formerly known as Ed)

#126: Cupcake for Victoria Gadsdon of Victoria's Kitchen

Caveman, Doctor Who & Mr Tumble (Halloween 2010)

#132: Highland Cow
for Gordon Edwards

That morning alone, Jack's donation total went up by
£3,000 as his piece appeared on national BBC Breakfast
and BBC News 24 all day. At one point, Jack was getting three
emails every minute! Dad tallied up the donations: 306
donations = 306 drawings, raised £5,295.34. Jack had done
23 drawings, but he was only six. He still had to go to school,
get his sleep and play. Everyone could only do their best.

A couple of days later, it was all still happening. Jack
had a photo-shoot for the first official press release, plus
follow-up interviews with the *East Lothian Courier*,
Edinburgh Evening News and the BBC. Jack only did one
picture, and then had an early night. He deserved it.

Jack #72

I didn't appreciate that I was one of the first people to donate and ask for a drawing. The rocket was actually my girlfriend Maarit's random idea, so I asked for it as a surprise for her.

- Kieren Jones

Jack #65

This was for my good friend Roger. Roger
isn't his real name. It's Ian, but his last name
sounds a bit like Ramjet, and so from the
time he was young, all his mates called him
Roger Ramjet. Roger had just been taken
into hospital with a horrible superbug and I
thought a Jack drawing would cheer
him up. - Andre

Ten days after the project started, the newly formed "Team Hendo" (Team Henderson) decided to set a deadline. Jack couldn't go on drawing pictures for ever! For Jack to actually finish all of the pictures anytime before Christmas, it made sense to stop taking requests exactly two weeks after we opened up the requests. People only had five days left to get their requests in – and the donation total was approaching £10,000. Was it possible to hit that target? STV News reran Jack's news piece with the story of the deadline, which meant even more donations and requests.

On April Fool's Day, Dad got a big shock while reading *Metro* on the train to work. And it wasn't a joke! He opened up the paper on the crowded North Berwick to Edinburgh train and found Jack staring back at him. He was so excited he told the woman sitting next to him!

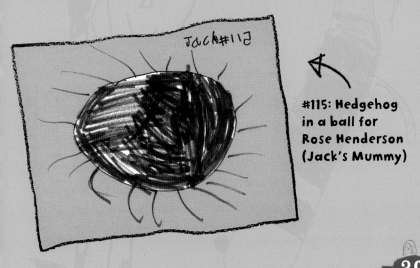

#115: Hedgehog in a ball for Rose Henderson (Jack's Mummy)

Two weeks after starting Jack's idea, he was so close to £10,000. Mum and Dad thought it would be amazing if they could get all the way there in two weeks. That night, Dad cheekily posted on Facebook for any secret millionaires to help out. A few donations came in, but they still hadn't made it.

Then a message popped up on Dad's computer screen from a friend, comedian and local good guy Scott Glynn. Lit up by the glow of the computer screen, Mum could see the smile grow across Dad's face as he read it. She knew it was good news! Scott had pledged the exact amount (£172.48) to take the total to exactly £10,000!

So there they were. Jack had done it! At 10.30pm, two weeks in, on Mothers' Day he had raised £10,000. Dad wanted to wake Jack up to tell him but Mum wouldn't let him.

Without telling Mum, Dad sneaked in to Jack's room when Mum nipped to make a cup of tea. Jack was asleep, of course, but Dad told him the news. He was too asleep to understand, and just grumbled and rolled over back to sleep.

#137: Dragonfly (farting flames to toast a normal fly) for Sarah Wiles

#71: Comedian Scott Glynn in Hawaiian shirt, shorts & crocs, with his golden labradors Charlie & Cody, featuring additional Ross High RFC coloured rugby ball and pint of beer on head, for Scott Glynn

Jack
#71

hack
hack

LONGEST TITLE

"I am proud to help a very special boy help a very special charity. At six you are wiser than most big people. Lots of love, Elaine."

Donation by Elaine Speirs

41

Hi Jack! If it's not a bother, I would like a picture of my friend Brian dancing like a crazy man. (If it helps, my friend Brian is extremely bald). P.S. Don't worry about the time, put this to the end of the queue if you like. He will still be bald whenever you draw him. Thanks a bunch. Ben.

In the morning Mum and Dad told a more awake Jack. He was super excited and was jumping on the couch with his little brothers. Once they all calmed down he was so keen to get to school to tell his teacher and all his friends.

The "well dones" and "congratulations" flooded in and before they knew it Jack was in the news again. Rather than feeling like an ending, hitting the £10,000 target was almost a new beginning.

Team Hendo felt like raising any money for charity was great. Raising £100 was amazing, £1000 was brilliant, but reaching £10,000 felt like an exclusive club. It almost seemed like just the accomplishment of raising that much meant that more and more people wanted to donate. It was a good day.

#67: Mr Potato Head riding an elephant, eating banana ice cream on a seesaw with a purple gorilla for Richie Gilbert

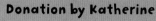

"What a huge achievement for a small boy - an inspiration to all!"

Donation by Katherine

Jack On TV

The next day, STV came back to the house before school to film a little piece about hitting the £10,000 target. Toby and Noah pulled out the cute card for this one, keen to be in front of the camera and showing off.

The excitement of reaching his total plus appearing in his school spring show as a hedgehog wore Jack out, and in true six-year-old style he was a little grumpy! So, Jack popped the pens away for the day and he went to have a lie down on the sofa and watch some cartoons instead. In his words, "I won't let my people down. I just need a wee rest!" No news, no computer, no visitors, just a lovely few hours off from the madness – and Team Hendo decided from then on to have one day off every week, to give Jack a chance to miss drawing and enjoy what he was doing. But he was back doing drawings the very next day ... like this one.

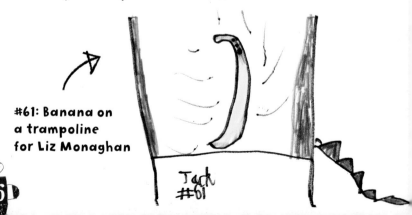

#61: Banana on a trampoline for Liz Monaghan

Jack #61

Jack#7P

My son Steven broke his leg and was in traction in the Sick Kids Hospital for ten days. Steven is a huge Star Wars fan and knew Jack could make Darth Vader look awesome.

Jack #7E

"You have oodles of creativity and your enthusiasm and spirit is really heart-warming. Thank you for bringing a smile to my day! Good luck!"

Donation by Joanne Calley

The day Jack's story had been on STV news Dad had received a telephone call from a researcher wondering if they would like to appear and draw on *The Hour*. *The Hour* is an evening chat show in Scotland presented by (former Pop Idol contestant) Michelle McManus and Stephen Jardine. Everyone was very excited and it meant being on LIVE TV!

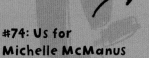

#74: US for Michelle McManus and Stephen Jardine (*The Hour*, STV)

8th April - *The Hour* (in Jack's words)

On Friday I went on a trip to Glasgow because I was going to go on *The Hour*. I had to get two trains and one taxi to get there as it is very far away.

I got to have a go at the driver bits on the train. I got to do the whistle and it went hooonnnnkkkk hooonnnnkkkk. This was before the train went from the station.

The train was fun. I drew a ninja fighting a pirate; the pirate's ear got cut off.

49

When I got to Glasgow Daddy and me got a taxi and I took a picture out of the window of a pretty building.

When we got to STV, there were lots of things to take pictures of. I took a picture of a BIG green crane for Toby.

Daddy let me stand on the big S. It was fun and I was trying to play leapfrog over them but my daddy told me to stop.

We went into the building and I met some people who were very nice and gave me a snack - they gave me crisps, Haribo, two big cakes and some Diet Coke. It was yummy. Then I went up to look in the room and I got a shot of the big news desk. I was reading out the weather and I said it was going to be Jack today!

We went back into the waiting bit where I got to sign a big desk with lots of other famous people.

I got to write beside the Krankies! I saw the Krankies at Christmas when we went to see John Barrowman in *Aladdin*. They were very silly and funny. I like them as Jimmy Krankie was hitting John Barrowman on the head and making me laugh.

#68: Sheep for Carl Shapiro

50

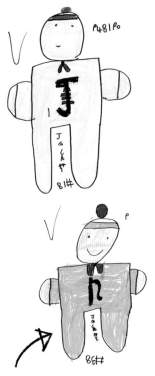

#82: Something that makes you happy (Rainbow Baby Red) for Laura Ketteridge

#83: Rainbow Baby Blue for Tommy & Lilian

I knitted the Rainbow Babies to help fundraise for the Sick Kids. Jack, Toby and Noah loved the babies so much I gave them one each. As a thank you to me, young Jack drew them and put them on his website. – Lilian Graham

Jack standing on the big S

Jack got to have a go with the whistle

Jack with Stephen Jardine and Michelle McManus

Jack reading out the news at STV

Jack #220

"What an inspirational boy for a great cause! My little girl was in the Sick Kids for about 5 months until the start of this year and they do a fantastic job."

Donation by Samantha Wallace

The real Dean O'Dinosaur!

JACK'S BIGGEST FAN

Jack #84

Deano is the biggest fan of the band Hayseed Dixie and has travelled to many of their gigs. As a result he has his own Facebook page. I thought Jack might like to draw Deano, as he has a flair for dinosaur portraits. - John

#49: Scottish countryside with the Loch Ness Monster for Jeanette, Charlie and Niamh

My daddy got make-up on. He looked very silly - only mummies put make up on!

The lady was pretending to put make-up on me, but she actually did put some on me.

When I was on *The Hour* it was funny. I liked looking at myself on the TV and I drew super quick. They gave me lots and lots of nice pens and paint. It was really nice.

At the end I got my picture taken with Stephen and Michelle. I liked every single one of them the best as they were so nice to me and instead of putting their money from their lunch in their pocket, they put it in a big box for me to take back to the Sick Kids Friends Foundation and helped me raise more than £11,000 which is very nice.

We had to leave and say goodbye; I was sad to go. We had to get our train.

Right before we went on air we got a call from Channel 4 to ask us to go on *Fern*, another chat show. We would be off to London!

#92: Doctor Who's Tardis for Louise Dryburgh

#10: Husband David dressed as Dr Who for Natalie Lees

DR WHO PICTURES

#135: The Silence (Doctor Who alien monster) for me (Jack Henderson)

#269: Weeping Angels (from Doctor Who) playing catch with the sun for Janet King

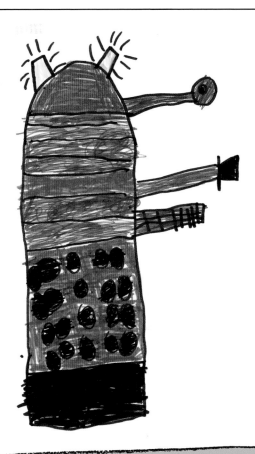

"Jack, you are one awesome little man.
Just keep doodling!"

Donation by Sharon Barrett

J ack #P8

**Well Done, Jack! Rock On!
Love, Brian**

- Brian May, Queen guitarist

CHAPTER 4

Doodle
Pages

Here are some pages for YOU
to draw on, with suggestions from
Jack. If you want to scan your
drawing and email it to
me@jackdrawsanything.com
it might end up on Jack's website:
jackdrawsanything.com

Draw your favourite animal!

#273: Sonic the Hedgehog for Gail & Willie

Jack says:
My favourite is a hedgehog. Toby likes rhinos and dinosaurs. Noah likes cats. Draw yours.

Draw something that is yellow!

#32: The Sun for Adrian Hilton

Jack says: Yellow is my favourite colour because it is really really bright.

Draw some bugs!

#124: 7 legged spider for
Carolyn Hicks husband
(we didn't know his name)

Jack says:
Bumblebees are
my favourite little
bugs. Big bugs are
good, too.

Draw your favourite meal!

#214: Your favourite dinner (chicken fajitas with guacamole, salsa & cheese and chocolate milkshake with straw) for Sarah

Jack says: My favourite meal is fajitas cause I like nice cheese and cream. **Yum!**

Draw your hobby!

#179: Jack's Mummy & Daddy doing judo for Kenny Graham (Jack's judo teacher)

Jack says: My hobby is judo. I like to do judo with Kenny. He is my teacher. Draw something you like to do.

Draw your family!

#5: Jack, Toby and Noah singing in bed while Daddy tells us off which makes us laugh for Melanie Russell of tictoc

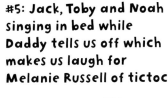

Jack says:
I have 2 brothers, Toby & Noah. Try to draw your brothers or sisters. If you don't have any, draw yourself!

65

Draw your favourite thing from TV!

#110: **Two Ood (Doctor Who aliens) in a kayak going different ways using their spheres as paddles for Debbie Happell of KAYAK**

Jack says: My favourite is Doctor Who because he is a time traveller.

Draw your house!

#91: House with a For Sale sign at the front for the ESPC

Jack says: This is my house. Draw yours and your street, too, if you have room.

After Jack had been on TV, everybody knew who Team Hendo was! Later that week, a package of donated art supplies arrived simply addressed to "Jack Draws Anything, Prestonpans" without any street name or postcode. The local sorting office was so wonderful that they knew EXACTLY where to deliver it!

Next stop, the Fern Britton show...

It took a whole day travelling on the train to get to London, and the next day Jack and his brothers were out of bed super early, excited about the adventures that were in store. Mum and Dad took them to the Natural History Museum. Toby was a huge fan of dinosaurs so they headed off to see what the museum held. The animated T-Rex was everyone's favourite. The kids had a fantastic time and needed an afternoon of rest in the hotel in South Kensington, while Mum and Dad had a little secret first meeting with Sara, our publisher!

#105: Otter sunbathing with sunglasses and a glass of lemonade with an umbrella in for Rory Fitzpatrick

Jack #107

Jack #1011

"Jack, you make the world a better place. **GOOD FOR YOU.** Don't over do it. **PLAY LOTS!** The world needs more 'Jacks'. Very best wishes, Gina Long, Suffolk."

SECOND PLACE

JACK #162

JACK #87

This illustration won the clash of the dinosaurs at netmums.com with a roaring 40% of the vote. (A close second was #162 Ninja (with added crossbow) riding on a Dinosaur for Douglas Sutherland.)

At 6pm, the big people carrier with blacked-out windows arrived and Toby fell asleep on the way as his bed time was normally 6.30pm. The whole family arrived at the TV studio and were shown to a private dressing room. Jack introduced himself with his usual catchphrase, "Hi, I'm Jack from Jack Draws Anything!"

When it was time for the filming to start, the whole family sat on the sofas as Fern did her introductions. It was lucky that it wasn't a live show, because the boys were very excited by it all. As the family were introduced, Toby sat and picked his nose and handed the bogey to Mum, while Noah attempted to escape and poor Jack got huge stage fright. Then, during Rhod Gilbert's interview, Noah kept roaring at him like a dinosaur and had to be removed from the set.

Roar!

JACK# 201

#207: Ladybird
for Lorraine Murray
(via Alison Denham)

Jack with Natalie Cassidy (Sonia from EastEnders)

Team Hendo after the show with Fern

With their favourite comedian Rhod Gilbert

JACK #247

"Good work, Jack. Sorry it can't be more money. Maybe one day when you're at art school, you'll know what it's like to be a poor student!"

Donation by Craig Young

#130: Giraffe for
Chris Bell and
Nick Hilditch
(@irkafirka)

It was soon decided that Team Hendo should go into
the green room and finish Jack's picture for Natalie
Cassidy (Sonia from *EastEnders*), which was a baby
playing a trumpet in a black cab. As he was leaving the set,
Toby ran over to the audience, roaring at them like a
dinosaur. He was loving the attention and had great fun.

When they were called back to the set to do the
interview, it was 8pm and everyone was pretty tired.
Jack got a bit of stage fright – he didn't want to answer.
Jack and Toby even managed to have a little argument on
air without anyone noticing. (Toby wanted to share the
pens!) They arrived back home in Scotland the next day
just in time to catch *Fern* – the kids loved watching
themselves on TV and talking about the experience
they just had.

Jack#191

This picture is for Greg Page, formerly of
the Wiggles. Greg had to leave in 2006 due
to ill health. Jack is a big fan of them
and Greg. Greg asked for Jack to draw him
"singing with the Wiggles". Jack's
interpretation of this was to draw the
present day Wiggles AND Greg to create
a double yellow fantastic five!

Jack
#128

"Your pictures have made me smile every day."

Donation by Tara Benson

While all of this was going on, there were a few emails chasing picture requests. Some people were being impatient, waiting for their drawings. It made Mum and Dad feel quite sad that people were chasing their six-year-old boy. They tried to politely explain that Jack is only six and that he has more than four hundred pictures still to do – while still having a normal family life! There is only physically so much that he can do in between school, judo, Beavers and normal six-year-old stuff. But the polite responses didn't work. The same people kept demanding their pictures.

Jack's mum and dad were determined to protect Jack and ensure that the project stayed fun for him. He did no more drawing than he normally would do and there were some days he did none at all. The spirit of the project – a donation to a good cause – should have been enough for people to be patient. In the end, the incredible support and encouragement from everyone on the Internet completely outweighed the negativity of a few people.

#265: Boobycat sleeping inside a postbox for Dulcie, Charlie & Carrie Druce

Unfortunately, that was not the only stress they would have to deal with. After four months of not needing hospital treatment, Noah got out of bed and sounded chesty and wheezy. He needed extra puffs on an inhaler to help open up his airways. This seemed to do the trick, and when Daddy left for work at 7.30am Noah was bouncing on the sofa singing *Twinkle Twinkle Little Star*.

But by 8am Noah had taken a drastic turn for the worse. He couldn't stand up; he was panting; his skin was almost translucent; and he couldn't stop coughing and wheezing. Mum and his brothers rushed Noah to the hospital, and as soon as the triage nurse took his stats he was put on oxygen. It was utterly heartbreaking for Mum to watch their almost two-year-old son grab an oxygen mask and willingly place it against his mouth. He should have been pushing it away, but because he has been in hospital so many times, he had already learned that the oxygen mask was what makes him better. It was even more heartbreaking watching him repeat this with the nebuliser, which was even more uncomfortable for him.

Jack #22

#22: Robot Olympics for Luc Warner-Lee

78

JOCK #227

DANGER

Margaret asked for something that makes Jack smile. He thought about the thing that made his brothers and him laugh the most at the moment and the answer was Mr Bean.

"Noah is a lucky little guy to have such a thoughtful big brother like you!"

Donation by Jamie Moffat

Mum and Dad called for Jack and Toby to be collected by their grandparents so they could concentrate on Noah. He was assessed by doctors and checked by nurses. A cannula (big needle) was inserted into his foot (as they could not find any veins in his arm or hand) as he lay whimpering "ow ow ow ow". He had another chest X-ray and the doctors were deciding whether to admit him into High Dependency when he started to brighten up. Within thirty minutes he was trying to put his Mr Tickle wellies on over his hugely bandaged foot, still whimpering "ow" but this time with a little more energy.

Because he looked much brighter and his stats (oxygen levels in his blood) had improved, they decided to move him to ward six. The lovely nurses in the ward recognised Noah instantly – another wonderful yet sad moment when you realise how many times he has been admitted to the ward in his very short life.

#93: A train for Thomas Lindon (who is nearly 2)

#171: Dancing Hedgehogs in the disco with flashing lights please for LauraKay Bunnett

This picture is the request of the 3000 Facebook Fans Celebration Contest. From a list of almost 60 requests, we whittled Jack down, knockout stylie to get to this one. He really wanted to draw them all!

In the morning, Noah had a visitor as Jack popped in to cheer him up. Noah was really happy to see his biggest brother and squealed "DACK!" as soon as he saw his toothless grin. Jack had brought his drawing stuff and he did some drawing with Noah in the Sick Kids while they waited to be discharged – like this one...

#103: Doctor Who (Tenth Doctor aka David Tennant) being chased by a dinosaur (it's actually eating his coat) for Dave Woodley

Noah and his Mr Tickle wellies

Jack made a point of introducing himself to all the staff by his catchphrase – "Hello, I'm Jack from Jack Draws Anything!" And they all knew who he was already!

Later that day, Noah was able to go home. He wasn't well, but he was well enough to get out of the Sick Kids and home to his own toys and own bed. The first thing he did when he got home was play on the trampoline and ask for some Easter eggs!

Despite Noah being in hospital that week and chaos everywhere, Jack kept up his drawing and managed a total of 21 pictures. That made 120 pictures in five weeks (an average of 24 per week).

#120: Mace Windu (Lego Star Wars) for Zoe, Sam & Ollie

JACR#120

Jack#174

"Little things can have a big effect. Hope you're proud of what you have achieved in such a short time! Well done and keep it up!"
Donation by Chris Webb

JaLR #06

The real Alice! Isn't she beautiful?

Being a doting owner of an African pygmy hedgehog, Alice, we were keen to see what Jack's amazing imagination would come up with! Alice liked it so much that she wandered over to have a look at it.

Jack Around the World

One night, just over a month into the project, Dad was about to go to bed when the Internet went absolutely bonkers. Jack Draws Anything was suddenly everywhere and the donations were flying in. Facebook and Twitter were updating too quickly for Dad to follow what was going on. It turned out that Jack was on *Russell Howard's Good News* on BBC3. Dad was so excited that he woke up Mum. She wasn't happy at first but was OK once he explained why. The show was aired four times that week, and Dad's computer almost melted!

This proved something Dad had long suspected. Social networking was amazing and could do so much for connecting people and spreading news, but to actually raise money, TV was way more effective.

#170: Taj Mahal for Georgina Parker

Jack #177

"You have done more in your life than many will ever do. Keep dreaming up good ideas and helping others."

Donation by James McCue

JACK #180

I asked for this because my daughter Sophie was eight weeks old, so my world revolved around her! I thought it would be great to have a baby portrait with a lovely story behind it to tell her about when she grows up.

#281: Edinburgh Castle with some flowers for Michele Henry

A couple of nights later, Jack lost his first tooth (the big one at the front, look at the book cover!) and was excited to pop it in his tooth pillow made by Mum for the tooth fairy to come. As Dad tucked him in, they chatted about what size of penny the tooth fairy would leave.

In the morning, Jack woke his parents up squealing with delight when he found his £1 coin from the Tooth Fairy. He ran through to their bedroom, still in his Dr Who pyjamas with some serious bed hair and bounced onto their bed, clutching his shiny £1 coin.

"Look what the tooth fairy left for me!" he screeched with excitement. "I'm going to put it straight in the Sick Kids collection tin." Mum and Dad knew that Jack had worked hard at getting that tooth out; it had been wobbling for weeks and he had his eye on a new sweetie in the local newsagent's that cost exactly £1. So Mum and Dad decided to get him the sweetie and let Jack put his £1 in the tin.

The following week, Mum was approached in the school playground by Robert Bryson, the Chairman of Cockenzie & Port Seton Community Council. He had been keeping up to date with Jack's progress and wanted to ask if it would be OK for the council to honour Jack's work at the big local Gala Day that Saturday.

Mum phoned Dad as soon as Jack had gone into school. "Jack is going to get an award at the Gala Day!" Dad thought it would be a nice little mention. "It's not just that," Mum squealed. "At the crowning of the Gala Queen, they are going to present him with the Youth Achievement Award! He's the youngest person ever to get it and he will get a trophy!" Mum and Dad knew how much this would mean to Jack, and so they decided to keep it as a surprise. This wasn't a trip to far-off London or something surreal like being on TV. This was local people that Jack knew!

JAC#288

#288: Forth Road Bridge for Josie Perry

Jack had great fun doing this one. He and Daddy looked up all the planets. Jack was sad when Daddy explained about the scientists deciding that Pluto was no longer a planet. Jack asked how they managed to move it and could he visit.

Jack #121

The request was for "a picture of a penguin to give to my two grandsons Kieran and Ryan who live in Germany to remind them of me as I don't see them very often." Jack added 2 snowballs, one with a K and one with an R.

When the day of the gala arrived, Jack was in a grump. He had gone to judo that morning and hadn't won the weekly trophy. Then they had to rush around doing some errands, pick up his brothers from his grandparents and hurry down to the Gala Day. So it was pretty safe to say he wasn't a happy little guy.

#158: Turtles surfing on the EAC (from Finding Nemo) for Dylan Leif Fenn and his parents Aisha and Alex

When they arrived, they chatted to friends and made their way to the tent where the crowning of the Gala Queen took place. It started to pour with rain. Mum and Dad felt a little guilty as other people stood outside in the rain, while their family were ushered to reserved seats. Jack didn't for one minute wonder why he had seats and their friends didn't; he just squirmed and kept asking if he could go on the rides. Jack's friend Jacob, from school, was a pageboy in the gala and was sitting in front of them. "Hi Jack. You're doing really well with your fundraising," said Laura, Jacob's mum. Jack blushed and looked at his feet.

Soon the bagpipes started and the Gala Queen and entourage entered the tent. Another of Jack's classmates, Harris, was also a pageboy in the gala. "Harris, you look funny in a kilt!" he shouted over the bagpipes.

Then, he turned to Mum and said, "Mum, I want to be in the gala next year. I want to go up on stage."

Mum just smiled.

Jack with his trophy!

JACK #187

#157: Spiderman stuck in the bath for Eleanor Plackett

Jack #194

"This is the most awesome thing I've seen in a long time. You are a star. And well done raising so much money for such a brilliant cause."

Donation by Paul Leader

Jack has created a visionary master plan for the Elephant & Castle area of South London. His high-rise neo-Norman castle, topped with a exceedingly long trunked elephant (a glass lift tower, perhaps, or water slide?) would make a fantastic centrepiece for the area. As a gardener I'm sorry to see he's only provided a very small amount of green space, but the expanse of water surrounding it would be a tremendous replacement for what is currently a three-lane roundabout.

At the end of the ceremony, Robert Bryson came on stage to say a few words and present some trophies. By that point, Jack was fidgeting so much Mum was considering just standing outside. But then the moment came – as soon as they said Jack's name, his face lit up and he hurried up on stage to collect his trophy from the Gala Queen.

He was asked to say a few words, and Mum and Dad were a little worried. They had no idea what he was going to say, and hadn't prepared anything for a speech. Jack hadn't even known he was getting a trophy. The microphone was lowered, and he took a step forward. Dad put his hands over his eyes wondering what Jack was going to say.

"Thank you," he said, and smiled as the entire tent and the outside spectators burst into applause for him. Mum and Dad were incredibly proud and had a huge feeling of relief!

#173: Laughing Lion for Linda Kong's girls

#186: Surfing Ninjas for Andrew Ward

Out of everything that had happened so far in this fantastic journey, for Jack this was THE biggest deal. His classmates were there; his head teacher was there; his parents and grandparents were there. In addition, he was given, in front of them all, a huge shiny trophy. Jack had no concept of how many people had read his story, no grasp of the sheer amount of money he had raised. All he understood was that when he went to the local shop, people knew who he was and said nice things to him and his brothers.

Team Hendo felt like they had a huge amount of support from the local community in Cockenzie & Port Seton. It was astounding. The family didn't know many local people, only parents of other children. But through this experience they met so many interesting, incredible and friendly people that they would never have had the pleasure of meeting. Yet one more benefit of this amazing idea.

It seemed, though, that Jack's story hadn't just touched people close to home. Word had spread far and wide.

JACK #11P

See if you can spot which one is the mummy... (Hint, look at the toe nails.)

"The Sick Kids did a lot for me over 20 years ago now and its amazing to see you raising so much for them. Well done!"

Donation by James Mitchelmore

The first time Mum and Dad heard from Sara, the publisher, they were very excited, but they didn't tell Jack about the possibility of a book happening until it was official. Jack was very excited and happy. He opened his mouth, made a funny wibble-wibble noise and jumped up and down. But that was nothing compared to what happened when the book was announced to the public. The reaction was amazing, everyone wanted to know about it and the story was EVERYWHERE. The response on Facebook and the donations were fantastic. Jack was so happy that he could finally tell all his friends and family that he was going to write a book! Dad got to do a radio interview for Real Radio and the news story about the book spent the entire day on the main BBC News home page. The website visits and donations were incredible. Jack was super famous for twenty-four hours.

#197: Big fairy with big wings sitting on a toadstool wearing welly boots and eating cake for Evelyn Smith

It wasn't just the UK that got excited. Dad received a telephone call from a lady who said she was from BBC Brazil. Dad didn't even know there was a BBC in Brazil. They requested permission to translate the BBC article about Jack's book into Portuguese. They also asked for some of his pictures.

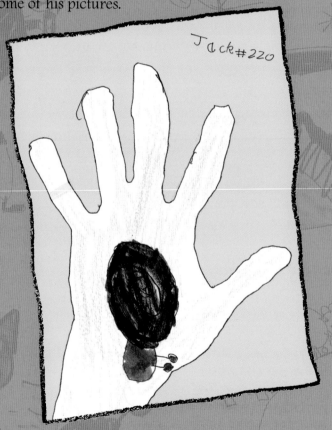

Jack#220

#220: A Giant African Landsnail sitting on a hand for Lindsey Welsh

#267 The Blackbird Diaries album cover
for Dave Stewart (@davestewart) - Artist/
Producer/Director & Eurythmics co-founder

Hi Jack from Jack Draws Anything. Thanks
so much for doing a drawing of my album
cover. You're doing a great job out
there! Keep at it! - Dave Stewart

"We could all learn a lesson from your big heartedness :)"

Donation by Lucy McCabe

#261: Pigeon with a shiny stone for Alex Gosling

JACK #261

Jack ended up being on the BBC Brazil homepage for the entire day, shown on BBC TV and was headline news on eight or nine main Brazilian websites. Jack also appeared on the front page of one of the main Brazilian newspapers. Dad was posting Facebook updates in Portuguese!

There had been support from Australia, Denmark, Taiwan, Germany ... all over. It seemed that the whole world loved Jack's story, but it wasn't over yet.

Jack #189

Lothian & Borders Fire & Rescue Service are our local fire brigade. Jack decided he wanted to draw them dealing with a big fire in our area and he thought the best/worst memorable thing to be on fire was Arthur's Seat.

Jack At Home

Every year, the Sick Kids Friends Foundation host the Teddy Toddle fundraiser where toddlers and younger kids do a wee lap of the Meadowbank athletics track in Edinburgh with their teddies and get sponsored! This year, Toby and Noah were asked to lead the race, right next to Spencer (from Balamory) and Nina (from Nina & The Neurons). Jack was very sad that he was too old to do the Toddle, but he was very happy to learn he would be in charge of starting it with a very loud air horn!

It was almost as if things had come full circle. Jack had done the Teddy Toddle as a toddler himself, and now that he had grown up, he had found a different and very special way of helping the Sick Kids – and people had noticed!

JACK #260

#260: Spencer from Balamory for Rodd Christensen (aka Spencer from Balamory)

Jack doing Teddy Toddle in 2006 with Da & Mum

#192: Happy 2nd Birthday Noah! Love Jack (enjoy your new trike) for Noah Henderson

Happy
Birthday
Noah

Jack age 2

21st May - Jack drew a picture of Noah on his new trike to say HAPPY BIRTHDAY. Noah is far too young to know what is happening but hopefully one day he will appreciate what Jack did and that he was involved.

"Awesome kid, awesome cause, feels great to donate."

Donation by Jono High

A few weeks into the project, the Sick Kids Friends Foundation had nominated Jack for the Scottish Charity Awards 2011 and Jack ended up being shortlisted.

Mum and Dad tried to explain to Jack what it meant – the category he was nominated for was the Charity Champion Award. There were five people in his group, and together they went through each person and what they had done for their respective charity.

"Wow," Jack said. "I don't think I could win. These people are amazing."

JAck #282

#252: Donkey (from Shrek) for Karin Lawes

Mum and Dad knew that Jack had only been fundraising for three months, while the other people nominated had devoted years of their lives to raising awareness for their cause, putting in lots of blood, sweat and tears.

Jack loved the lead-up to the awards. He was fitted for a tuxedo and chatted non-stop at school about the awards. He even convinced his teacher it was going to be on TV when it wasn't.

When the night of the awards arrived, Jack was treated like a mini-celebrity. Everyone knew who he was and what he had achieved, and they all wanted to say well done to him. He found it all a bit overwhelming at first, especially as there was an initial reception in a full-to-the-brim marquee. He hid in the corner, playing on Mum's iPhone, not wanting to chat to the strangers in the room. That was until he spotted someone familiar in the crowd that he didn't expect to be there – a mum of one of his classmates. She came over to make a fuss of him, telling him how smart he looked. It was the little confidence boost he needed and from there on he strutted around the awards like everyone was there to see him!

 Team Hendo with Jack's certificate

#251: Blue Ninja from Lego Ninjago for Anouchka Doondeea

"I would not like Jack to draw me a picture.
I would like him to put down his pencils for
10 mins and sit and watch his favourite
cartoon x x x x"

Donation by Jayne Walker

JACK #247

"Jack, you are the next Picasso!"
Donation by Catherine Spencer-Smith

He really enjoyed the evening. When they read out the shortlist for the awards, he thought he had won, and tried to make his way onto the stage! He was a little embarrassed, but when he heard that Laura Lee of Maggie's Cancer Centres had won he stood up on his seat and clapped the loudest. When he had first heard the list of nominees, Jack thought that she should really win the award.

But the committee still wanted to give him some special recognition. They called out his name and asked him to go up on stage. They had a little goodie bag for him, and he was over the moon. Edinburgh College of Art had kindly given Jack some drawing materials; Edinburgh Zoo had donated a family pass to the zoo; and his certificate had been framed for him. He was thrilled!

JACK IN THE FUTURE

So you may be thinking that after 300-odd pictures Jack is fed up of crayons, but nothing would be further from the truth. He still loves to draw and even when he is drawing a picture to raise funds, he is a happy chap who absolutely LOVES turning an idea into a finished picture.

#199: Tiger in the Jungle for Jay Selley

His drawing has improved so much in only a few months ~ you can really see if you go back to the first few drawings and compare them to later ones ~ and he is still keen to learn more. Every picture brings a new piece of knowledge or a new technique to try.

As his parents, we have done our best to protect him during this fundraising and we think we have done not too badly. Jack now understands a little bit more that life is not just about "take, take, take", "how much money?" and "celebrity". He realises that if everyone helps a little, it benefits everyone.

Regardless of what happens with this project in the future, Jack has done an amazing thing and we hope it has set him on the right path for the rest of his life and that he continues to grow up in the manner which he has done so far.

Lastly, Jack has an amazing thing to put on his CV and it makes me chuckle to think of him in a job interview (or trying to impress a potential girlfriend) with his well~worn catchphrase, "Hi, I'm Jack from Jack Draws Anything."

#202: Girl with antlers wearing a green dress for Laura Simms from Create as Folk

JACK #246

Jack and his brothers are huge fans of Parry Gripp and his amazing songs. Boogie Boogie Hedgehog is probably their absolute favourite, but they still **LOVE** Cat Flushing the Toilet.

This picture won the Facebook Cat Fight!
Perhaps it was the Whovians...? Thanks to
everyone who voted. (www.facebook.com/
jackdrawsanything)

Thank you Miss Manson you have been a lovely teacher. Here is a little surprise for you for being the best teacher in the world.

- Jack

JACK#117

Anne was the person who first purchased a picture from Jack, and her son George is the other person in the fire engine in picture #11 on page 16.

Thank you!

FROM MUM & DAD

We have many people that we would like to thank for their help and support. We have done our best to remember and thank everyone, but if we have missed you out, please don't take it personally. It really is because Dad is the most forgetful man on the planet (and Jack has his genes).

All of the staff and pupils at Cockenzie Primary School, in particular Jack's Primary 2 teacher, Fiona Manson. Without her encouragement, support and fantastically good nature Jack would never have contemplated a project of this size.

Maureen, Rachel and all of the Sick Kids Friends Foundation team for their constant support.

Thank you so much to all of the staff and volunteers at The Royal Hospital for Sick Children in Edinburgh. Thanks to the staff in A&E for being so professional, reassuring and thorough during the many trips through your doors - without your swift and professional action we would not have Noah with us now. Thank you to Julie Westwood and all of the other staff in the asthma clinic for being so patient and answering our many, many questions, plus ensuring Noah's three-monthly check ups are as much fun as possible for him. The biggest thank you goes to Linda Smith and all of the staff on Ward 6. Their kind words, hard work and wonderful care make Noah's many visits easier to cope with.

Liz Monaghan and Steve Kydd at STV, Gavin Walker at BBC, Kirsty Gibbins at the *East Lothian Courier* and the *Edinburgh News/Scotsman* team for their constant and excellent news reports which helped get the ball rolling, and kept it rolling.

Noah says THANK YOU in his own unique way!

"G'day Jack, from Australia! Your goodwill and kind spirit is reaching to the other side of the world. Keep it up, mate!"

Donation by Paul Carr

Jack
#224

Thank you!

The production teams at *The Hour*, *Fern*, *Russell Howard's Good News*, BBC News, STV News. You don't realise how much good you actually did by putting the wee man on the wee screen. Thank you so much.

Sara and all of the guys at Hodder Children's/Hachette for taking the plunge and offering a six-year-old boy a book deal!

Huge big thank you to Jacqui Low and Suzanne Mackie of Indigo PR in Edinburgh. They helped us deal with the press and media, and offered us invaluable advice when we had no idea what we were doing!

Dean O'Dinosaur for being Jack's BIGGEST fan (ROAR!) and all of the lovely people who have been so supportive on Facebook.

ALL of our family and friends for helping to spread the word about Jack and his wee project.

Everyone who took the time to donate, request a picture, send an email, send art supplies, tweet, write a letter, Facebook, LinkedIn, blog, news story and ultimately spread the word about Jack's work – without each and every person's support this book and the massive fundraising total would never have been possible.

Good luck Jack, Toby and Noah! From Murray, Jeff, Anthony, and Sam (The Wiggles)

FROM JACK

Thank you, Sara and all the other people in your work who have made my book. Thank you to everybody that donated. I have raised lots of money. Thank you, Dad, for doing my website. Thank you, Mum, for making my tea. Thank you, Toby and Noah, for being nice little brothers. Thank you, all my family, for helping me and donating, and hello to my cousins Ethan, Sam and Libby. Finished.

INDEX

#26: Number 26 bus with people on it and a bus driver for Matthew

Biography

Jack Henderson is a typical six-year-old who loves hedgehogs, *Doctor Who*, John Barrowman, judo and running around. He lives in East Lothian, Scotland, with his brother Toby (3), his brother Noah (2) and their mum and dad, Ed and Rose. They are a normal family. The boys rule the roost and Mum and Dad get by on minimal sleep.

Only Jack's first 290 pictures could make it into this book. If you want to see the rest, and find out what Jack and his family are up to these days, visit jackdrawsanything.com or facebook.com/jackdrawsanything.

#254: Jack with a BIG smile for Mark Singleton

Jack#254